Keys to the C...

Written by Lisa Thompson
Pictures by Andy and Inga Hamilton

It was late when the King came home from hunting. The castle doors were closed. He was locked out.

The King had promised he would not be late for dinner.

The Queen liked the family to all be on time for dinner.

"Oh dear," said the King. "I must have left my keys in my other cloak."

The King knocked on the door. No one answered.

He yelled out. No one came.

"How will I get in?" said the King. "I can't be late for dinner."

The King built a tower out of old boxes. He began to climb.

7

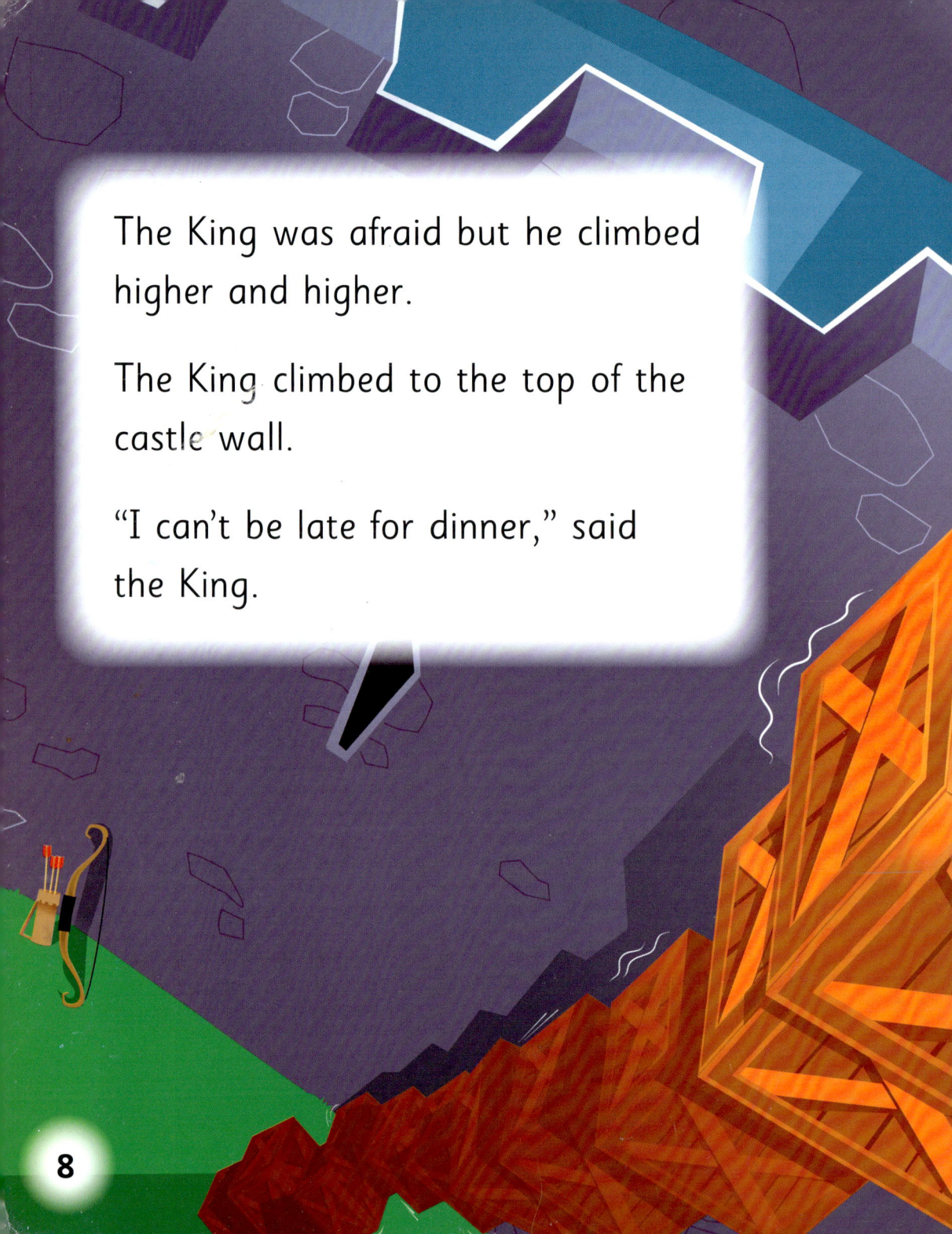

The King was afraid but he climbed higher and higher.

The King climbed to the top of the castle wall.

"I can't be late for dinner," said the King.

The only way down was to jump.

The King jumped down from the castle wall. He landed in the muddy pigpen.

"Oink! Oink! Oink!" squealed the pigs. They wanted him to stay and play.

"Not now," said the King.
"I can't be late for dinner."

The King ran across the royal garden.

Fang, the dog, chased the King.

"Woof! Woof! Woof!" barked Fang.

Fang wanted the King to stay and play.

"Not now, Fang," said the King.
"I can't be late for dinner."

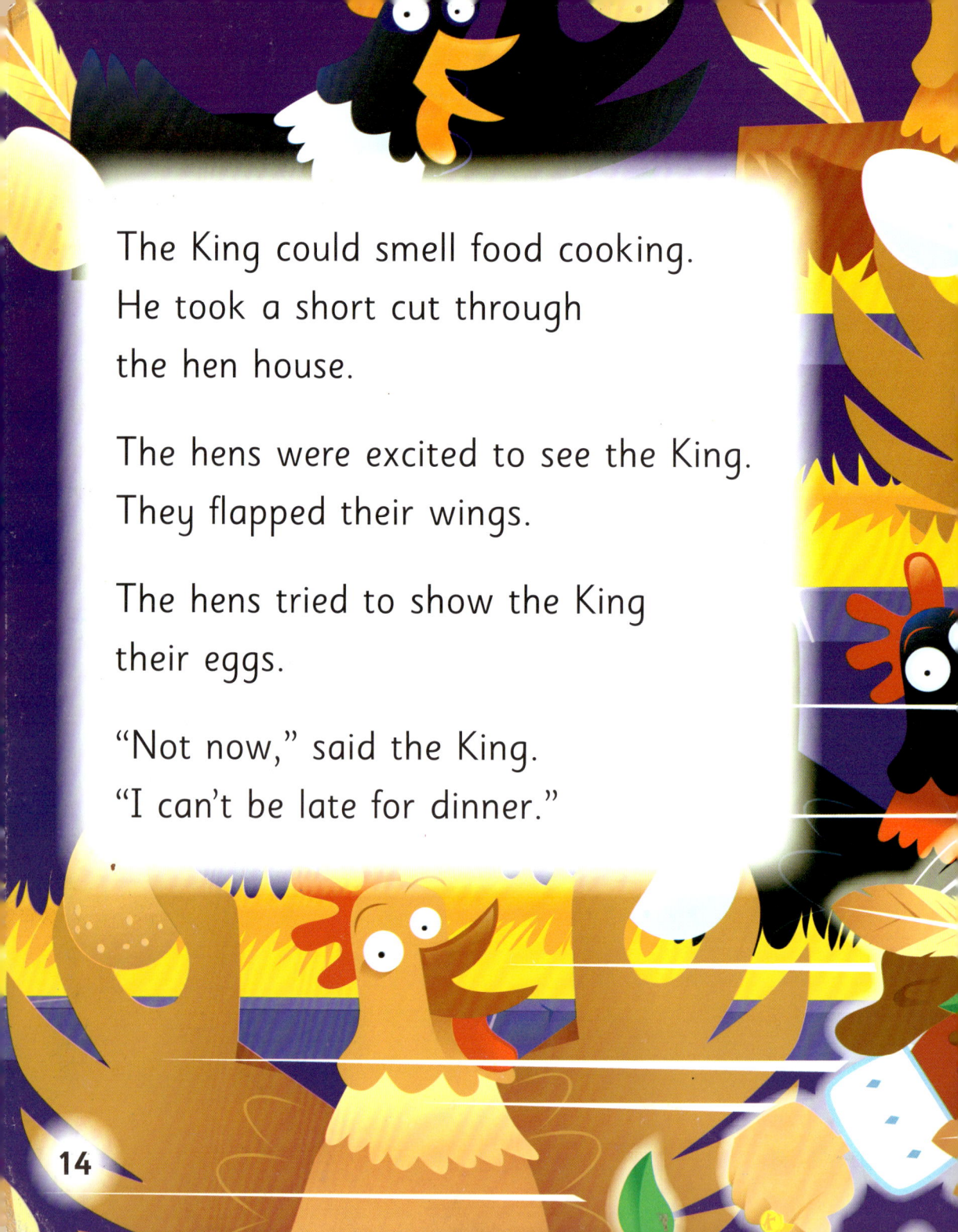

The King could smell food cooking. He took a short cut through the hen house.

The hens were excited to see the King. They flapped their wings.

The hens tried to show the King their eggs.

"Not now," said the King. "I can't be late for dinner."

The King made it into the castle. He ran to the dining room. He could hear laughter. Dinner was about to be served.

The King opened the dining room doors and ran in.

The Queen screamed.

"Help! Help!" the Princess cried.

"It's a wild beast!" yelled the Prince. "I shall catch it and throw it in the dungeon."

The guards waved their swords at the King.

"Stop, I am not a wild beast. I am the King!"

The Queen, Prince and Princess gasped.

The King washed his face and hands. The family sat down for dinner.

"I am very glad I am not late," said the King. "I am as hungry as a beast!"